REVISED EDITION

Lado Picture Dictionary

Robert Lado

Regents/Prentice Hall, Englewood Cliffs, NJ 07632

Library of Congress Cataloging-in-Publication Data

Lado, Robert, 1915–
    Lado picture dictionary / Robert Lado. — Rev. ed.
        p. cm.
    Includes index.
    ISBN 0-13-061680-X
    1. Picture dictionaries, English. 2. English language—Textbooks
for foreign speakers. I. Title.
PE1629.L33 1993
423′.1—dc20
                                    92–36959
                                        CIP

Editorial/Production Supervision: **Christine McLaughlin Mann**
Acquisitions Editor: **Tina B. Carver**
Development Editor: **Barbara Barysh**
Managing Editor: **Sylvia Moore**
Interior Art: **Len Shalansky**
Cover Design and Art Production: **Laura Ierardi**
Design Supervisor: **Christine Gehring-Wolf**
Contributing Artist: **Warren Fischbach**
Prepress Buyer: **Ray Keating**
Manufacturing Buyer: **Lori Bulwin**

© 1993 by REGENTS/PRENTICE HALL
A Division of Simon & Schuster
Englewood Cliffs, New Jersey 07632

Printed in the United States of America
10 9 8 7 6

ISBN 0-13-061680-X

Prentice-Hall International (UK) Limited, *London*
Prentice-Hall of Australia Pty. Limited, *Sydney*
Prentice-Hall Canada Inc., *Toronto*
Prentice-Hall Hispanoamericana, S.A., *Mexico*
Prentice-Hall of India Private Limited, *New Delhi*
Prentice-Hall of Japan, Inc., *Tokyo*
Simon & Schuster Asia Pte. Ltd., *Singapore*
Editora Prentice-Hall do Brasil, Ltda., *Rio de Janeiro*

CONTENTS

INTRODUCTION

A picture dictionary is a wonderful help to the student and the teacher in presenting many new words directly associated with their meaning through pictures in context. It is especially helpful if the teacher not only teaches words but leads the student to use them in conversation and to expand their number in order to communicate personal experiences and develop practical fluency.

The 114 picture pages in full color of the *Lado Picture Dictionary: Revised Edition* introduce more than 2800 words and provide the context and stimulus for many more words that are related to them as the student tries to express his or her experiences with the help and support of the teacher.

Lively pictures made more attractive with a touch of humor make the lessons more appealing and easier to remember. Using the words in context to communicate the thoughts of the students changes their attitude from a passive one of just trying to remember to a dynamic one of conveying what they intend to communicate. For example, learning the names of the parts of the body is important enough to learn English, but using them to identify persons by describing what they look like and what they are wearing is more compelling. It is necessary to know if the person is tall or short, fat or thin, blond or brunette, and if the hair is long or short, wavy or straight. To that end, the pictures illustrate adjectives to describe persons and verbs of things that one does with the hands, the head, the mouth, etc.

The *Lado Picture Dictionary: Revised Edition* lends itself to many classroom activities guided by the teacher, and the Workbooks are designed for individual work in class or assigned as homework. The students (1) identify the pictures by their names, (2) remember their names when looking at the pictures, (3) use the words in conversation and other activities led by the teacher, and (4) think of and ask the teacher for new words needed to tell their experiences in the same context.

This revised edition uses larger type to see and remember the words better, the numbers are easier to find, and art work was revised to better clarify the ideas and identify the items. We are sure that the revised edition will be clearer to the students as they try to identify items and relate to the picture stories.

Robert Lado

SELF AND FAMILY

BODY

1. head	**7.** arm	**13.** waist	**18.** shin
2. face	**8.** elbow	**14.** buttocks	**19.** leg
3. neck	**9.** wrist	**15.** hip	**20.** calf
4. shoulder	**10.** hand	**16.** thigh	**21.** ankle
5. back	**11.** stomach	**17.** knee	**22.** foot, feet
6. chest	**12.** abdomen		

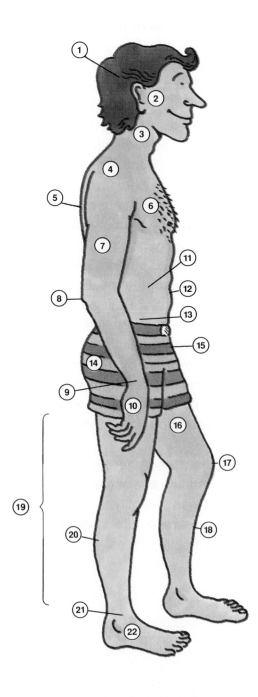

ORGANS AND SKELETON

Organs

1. brain
2. esophagus
3. throat
4. windpipe
5. spinal cord
6. lungs
7. heart
8. stomach
9. liver
10. spleen
11. kidney
12. pancreas
13. small intestine
14. large intestine
15. appendix
16. colon
17. bladder
18. artery
19. vein
20. blood
21. muscle

Skeleton

22. skull
23. cheek, cheekbone
24. jaw, jawbone
25. bones
26. neck
27. collarbone
28. ribs
29. breastbone
30. backbone
31. hip bone
32. thighbone
33. kneecap
34. shin
35. anklebone
36. shoulder blade
37. arm
38. forearm
39. hand

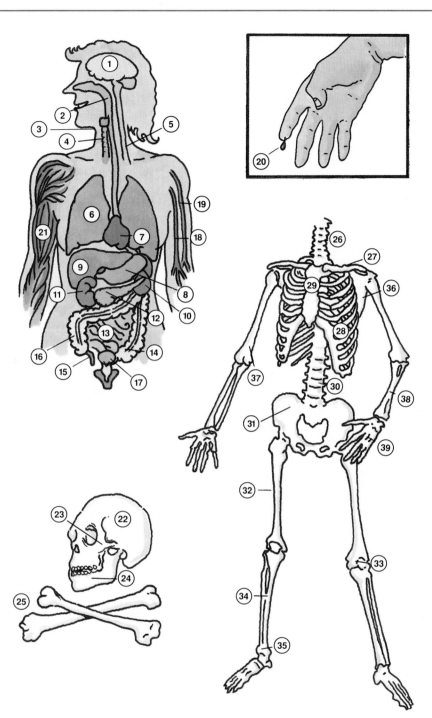

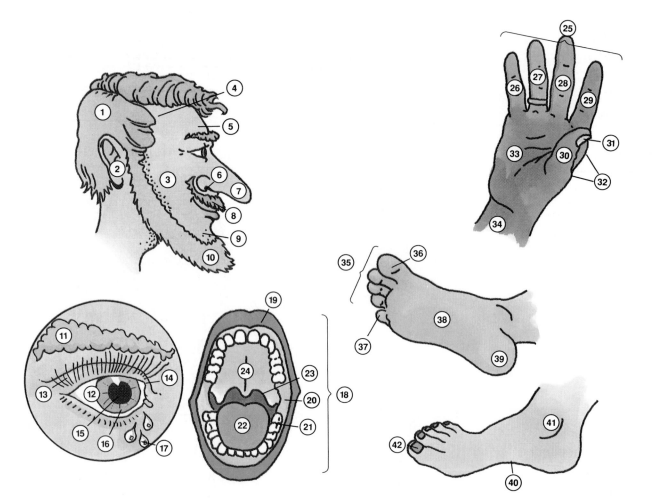

Face

1. hair
2. ear
3. cheek
4. temple
5. forehead
6. nostril
7. nose
8. mustache
9. chin
10. beard

Eyes

11. eyebrow
12. eye
13. eyelashes
14. eyelid
15. pupil
16. iris
17. tears

Mouth

18. mouth
19. lip
20. gum
21. tooth, teeth
22. tongue
23. tonsils
24. uvula

Hand

25. fingers
26. little finger
27. ring finger
28. middle finger
29. index finger
30. thumb
31. fingernail
32. knuckles
33. palm
34. wrist

Foot

35. toes
36. big toe
37. little toe
38. sole
39. heel
40. arch
41. ankle
42. toenail

RELATED VERBS

Ear
1. hear/listen

Eye
2. cry
3. look/see

Hand
4. write
5. point (to)
6. throw
7. wave

Head
8. think

Mouth
9. bite
10. drink
11. eat/taste
12. kiss
13. smile
14. speak/talk

Body
15. run
16. sit
17. stand
18. walk

Nose
19. smell

DESCRIBING PEOPLE: ADJECTIVES

1. tall
2. short
3. fat
4. thin
5. strong
6. weak
7. big
8. small
9. well
10. sick
11. beautiful
12. ugly

Hair

13. blond/blonde
14. brunette
15. long
16. short
17. wavy
18. curly
19. straight
20. bald

FAMILY

1. man ⎫ husband
2. woman ⎭ and wife
3. boy ⎫ brother and
4. girl ⎭ sister
5. baby
6. children
7 & 8 ⎫
9 & 10 ⎬ husband and
11 & 12 ⎭ wife
7 & 10; 10 & 13, 14
   father & son(s)
8 & 11; 9 & 15;
   11 & 16, 17, 18
   mother &
   daughter(s)
10 & 11; 13, 14 & 15
   brother(s) &
   sister
8 & 9 mother-in-law &
   daughter-in-law
7 & 12 father-in-law &
   son-in-law
12 & 13, 14 uncle &
   nephew(s)
9 & 16, 17, 18 aunt &
   niece(s)
9, 10 & 13, 14, 15
   parents &
   children
7 & 13, 14 grandfather
   & grandson(s)
8 & 15, 16, 17, 18
   grandmother &
   granddaughter(s)
13, 14, 15, 16,
   17, 18 cousins

EMOTIONS

1. love
2. hate
3. admiration
4. disgust
5. pride

6. shame
7. happiness
8. grief
9. confidence
10. distrust

11. tenderness
12. joy
13. anger
14. sadness
15. pity

16. envy
17. surprise
18. fear
19. shock
20. depression

2 CLOTHING AND COLORS

OUTER CLOTHING

1. umbrella
2. crewneck sweater
3. sleeve
4. lapel
5. raincoat

6. boots
7. hat
8. zipper
9. jacket
10. shoes
11. cap
12. V-neck sweater

13. overcoat
14. scarf
15. pocket
16. button
17. shoelace
18. uniform
19. coat

20. rain boots
21. earmuffs
22. turtleneck
23. down vest
24. mittens
25. jeans
26. hiking boots

MEN'S CLOTHING

1. suit
2. suit jacket
3. shirt
4. collar
5. tie
6. vest
7. handkerchief
8. belt
9. buckle
10. pants
11. cuff
12. briefcase
13. sport coat
14. sport shirt
15. slacks
16. loafer(s)
17. heel
18. sole
19. sneakers
20. bathrobe
21. pajamas
22. slipper(s)
23. glasses
24. wallet
25. money

Underwear

26. underpants/briefs
27. undershirt/T-shirt
28. boxer shorts
29. long johns

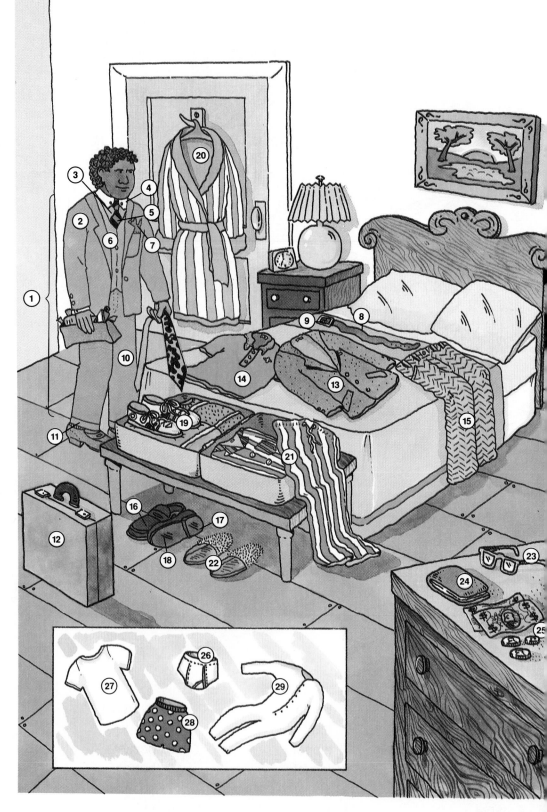

WOMEN'S CLOTHING

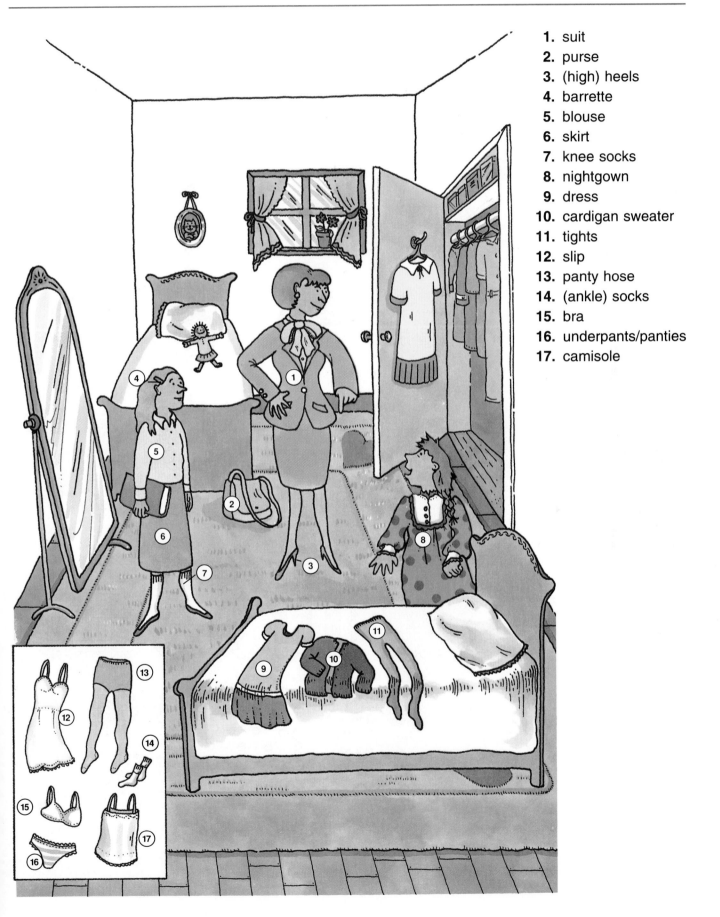

1. suit
2. purse
3. (high) heels
4. barrette
5. blouse
6. skirt
7. knee socks
8. nightgown
9. dress
10. cardigan sweater
11. tights
12. slip
13. panty hose
14. (ankle) socks
15. bra
16. underpants/panties
17. camisole

COLORS AND PATTERNS

Colors

1. red (apple)
2. orange (orange)
3. yellow (sun)
4. green (frog)
5. blue (eyes)
6. purple (grapes)
7. turquoise (ring)
8. pink (piggy bank)
9. tan (sand castle)
10. gray (mouse)
11. brown (chair)
12. black (tire)
13. beige (bandage)
14. white (snowman)
15. gold (bracelet)
16. silver (coins)

Patterns

17. solid
18. striped
19. checked
20. plaid
21. paisley
22. polka dot
23. flower print

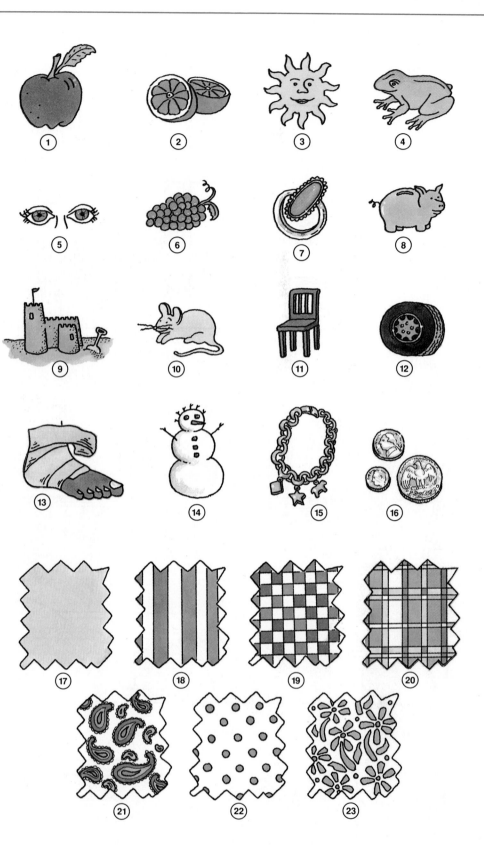

JEWELRY, COSMETICS, TOILETRIES

Jewelry

1. pearls
2. engagement ring
3. tie clip
4. ring
5. bracelet
6. chain
7. necklace
8. watch
9. watchband
10. cufflinks
11. clip-on earring

12. pierced earring
13. pin
14. clasp
15. wedding ring

Cosmetics

16. make-up table
17. cotton balls
18. eye shadow
19. eyeliner
20. mascara
21. eyebrow pencil

22. blush/rouge
23. lipstick
24. powder
25. make-up brush

Toiletries

26. hair dryer
27. razor
28. comb
29. hair brush
30. bobby pins
31. curlers

32. electric shaver
33. shaving cream
34. razor blades
35. soap
36. perfume
37. after-shave lotion
38. nail polish
39. emery board
40. nail clipper
41. tweezers
42. shampoo

HOUSE AND HOME

HOUSING

1. mansion
2. swimming pool
3. lamp post
4. driveway
5. apartment building
6. condominium
7. balcony
8. parking place
9. function room/
   club house
10. townhouse
11. street
12. sidewalk

13. adobe house
14. colonial house
15. mailbox
16. ranch house
17. lawn
18. cottage/bungalow
19. fence
20. mobile home

Outside

1. yard
2. garage
3. driveway
4. street
5. sidewalk
6. fence
7. gate
8. steps
9. porch
10. doorbell
11. door
12. window
13. shutters
14. roof
15. chimney
16. antenna

Inside

17. attic
18. bedroom
19. bathroom
20. nursery
21. kitchen
22. dining room
23. stairs
24. closet
25. hall/foyer
26. floor
27. living room
28. family room/den
29. basement
30. laundry room
31. tool room/ workshop

1. window	**9.** closet	**17.** piano	**24.** sofa/couch/divan
2. curtains	**10.** front door	**18.** piano bench/	**25.** coffee table
3. shades/blinds	**11.** lock	piano stool	**26.** armchair
4. mantel	**12.** coat rack	**19.** wood/log	**27.** footstool
5. fireplace	**13.** handrail	**20.** hearth	**28.** telephone
6. clock	**14.** stairs	**21.** carpet/rug	**29.** end table
7. painting/picture	**15.** staircase	**22.** rocking chair	**30.** telephone book/
8. light switch	**16.** plant	**23.** vase	directory

KITCHEN

1. refrigerator
2. ice tray
3. freezer
4. cabinet
5. microwave oven
6. dishcloth
7. faucet
8. sink
9. dishwasher
10. garbage disposal
11. dish towel
12. dish drainer
13. window sill
14. window
15. table
16. chair
17. cutting board
18. tea kettle
19. sauce pan
20. lid
21. stove/range
22. pot
23. handle
24. pot holder
25. oven
26. blender
27. broiler
28. wastebasket
29. stool
30. frying pan/skillet
31. colander
32. whisk
33. counter top/
    counter
34. (electric) mixer
35. mixing bowl
36. can opener
37. canister
38. rolling pin

1. picture
2. frame
3. ceiling light
4. china cabinet/ cupboard
5. china
6. buffet/sideboard
7. saucer
8. cup
9. teapot
10. sugar bowl
11. creamer
12. coffee pot
13. chair
14. table
15. napkin
16. glass
17. salad bowl
18. napkin ring
19. pitcher
20. pepper shaker
21. salt shaker
22. fork
23. candle
24. candlestick
25. casserole dish
26. spoon
27. plate
28. bottle
29. bottle opener
30. knife
31. tablecloth

1. bed	**11.** comforter/	**19.** closet	**28.** window
2. headboard	down quilt	**20.** dresser	**29.** curtain
3. bedspread	**12.** night stand/	**21.** mirror	**30.** air conditioner
4. pillow	night table	**22.** drawer	**31.** floor
5. pillowcase	**13.** lamp	**23.** wall	**32.** hairbrush
6. flat sheet	**14.** lamp shade	**24.** door	**33.** comb
7. fitted sheet	**15.** alarm clock	**25.** doorknob	**34.** bureau/
8. blanket	**16.** picture	**26.** light switch	chest of drawers
9. mattress	**17.** frame	**27.** ceiling	**35.** carpet
10. box spring	**18.** shelf		

NURSERY

1. crib
2. bars
3. bumper
4. blanket
5. baby/infant
6. pacifier
7. bottle
8. nipple
9. mobile
10. toy chest
11. swing
12. stroller
13. baby wipes
14. high chair
15. baby powder
16. doll
17. changing table
18. changing pad
19. baby lotion
20. cloth diaper
21. playpen
22. bib
23. stuffed animal/
     teddy bear
24. walker

1. bath mat
2. bathtub
3. drain
4. soap dish
5. soap
6. washcloth
7. sponge
8. stopper
9. scale

10. tile floor
11. clothes hamper
12. bath towel
13. hand towel
14. towel rack
15. shower
16. shower curtain
17. shower head

18. curtain rod
19. curtain rings
20. ceiling fan/
    ventilator
21. wallpaper
22. toilet paper/tissue
23. toilet
24. light

25. mirror
26. medicine cabinet/
    chest
27. toothbrush
28. toothpaste
29. sink/basin
30. faucet
31. glass

1. washer/washing machine	9. fabric softener	18. hot water heater	27. bucket/pail
2. dryer	10. laundry detergent	19. furnace/boiler	28. clothesline
3. ironing board	11. electric panel	20. water meter	29. vacuum cleaner
4. iron	12. electric meter	21. clothespin	30. workbench
5. extension cord	13. paint cans	22. sump pump	31. brush
6. outlet	14. smoke detector	23. fuel tank/oil tank	32. laundry
7. plug	15. sandpaper	24. (dust) mop	33. laundry basket
8. bleach	16. roller	25. (sponge) mop	34. broom
	17. paintbrush	26. ladder	35. dustpan

YARD

1. deck
2. grill/barbecue
3. charcoal
4. lighter fluid
5. flower bed/
   flower garden
6. vegetable garden
7. patio
8. patio chair
9. patio table
10. umbrella
11. lawn/grass
12. shrub/bush
13. hose
14. swimming pool
15. diving board
16. lounge chair
17. tree
18. hedge
19. wheelbarrow
20. toolshed
21. rake
22. shovel
23. lawn mower

VERBS

1. welcome
2. knock
3. ring (the bell)
4. visit
5. answer (the door)
6. answer (the phone)
7. go upstairs
8. go downstairs
9. lock the door
10. turn on the lights
11. turn off the lights
12. clean
13. vacuum
14. sweep
15. dust
16. fix/repair
17. mow
18. paint

FRUIT

1. apple
2. apricot
3. banana
4. blueberries
5. blackberries
6. raspberries
7. cranberries
8. strawberries
9. raisins
10. cantaloupe
11. honeydew melon
12. watermelon
13. cherries
14. (a bunch of) grapes
15. fig
16. coconut

17. grapefruit
18. orange
19. lime
20. lemon
21. pineapple
22. guava
23. kiwi
24. mango
25. papaya
26. pear
27. nectarine
28. peach
29. plum
30. persimmon
31. pomegranate
32. quince
33. prickly pear

VEGETABLES

1. cabbage
2. brussels sprouts
3. collard greens
4. kale
5. spinach
6. lettuce

7. tomatoes
8. carrots
9. radish
10. avocado
11. cauliflower

12. lima beans
13. broccoli
14. potatoes
15. sweet potatoes/ yams

16. (ear of) corn
17. string beans/ green beans
18. chickpeas/ garbanzo beans

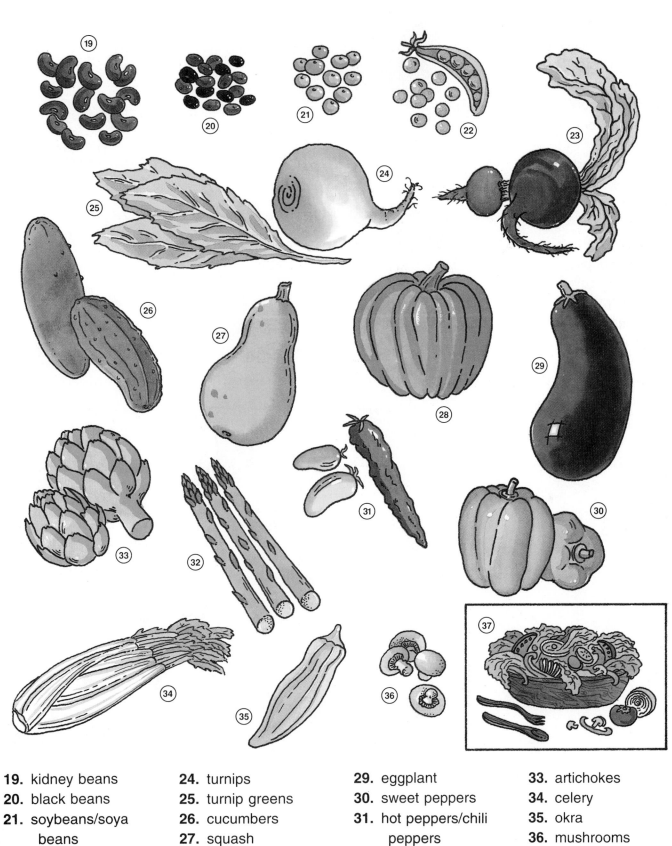

19. kidney beans	**24.** turnips	**29.** eggplant	**33.** artichokes
20. black beans	**25.** turnip greens	**30.** sweet peppers	**34.** celery
21. soybeans/soya beans	**26.** cucumbers	**31.** hot peppers/chili peppers	**35.** okra
22. green peas	**27.** squash	**32.** asparagus	**36.** mushrooms
23. beets	**28.** pumpkin		**37.** (bowl of) salad

MEAT

1. beef (cow/steer)
2. steak/beefsteak
3. T-bone steak
4. sirloin steak
5. filet mignon/
   tenderloin
6. roast
7. hamburger/ground
   beef
8. spare ribs
9. liver
10. pork (pig)
11. pork chops
12. bacon
13. ham
14. sausage
15. lamb
16. lamb chops
17. hot dog/
   frankfurter/wiener
18. cold cuts
19. bologna
20. salami

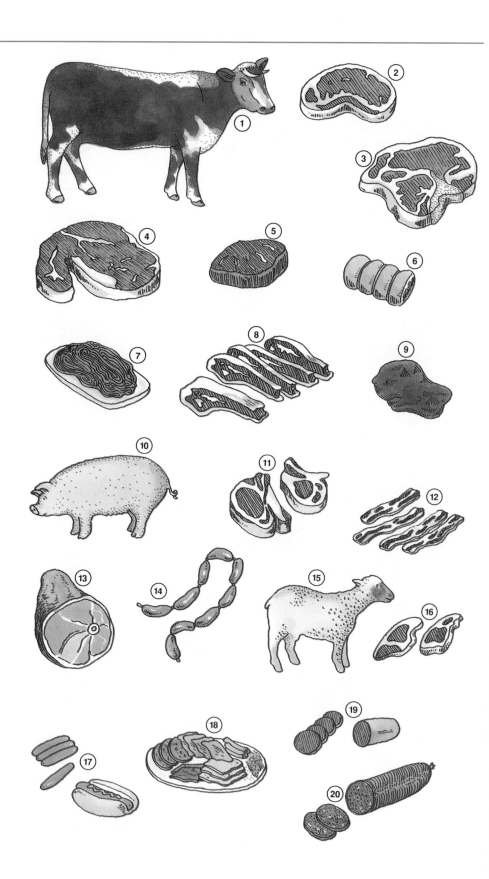

POULTRY AND SEAFOOD

Poultry
1. chicken
2. turkey
3. duck
4. hen
5. (whole) chicken
6. wing
7. thigh
8. leg/drumstick
9. breast
10. chicken filet
11. barbecued/grilled chicken

Fish
12. fish filet
    a. cod
    b. flounder
    c. haddock
13. steak
    a. halibut
    b. salmon
    c. tuna
14. red snapper
15. sardines
16. perch

Shellfish
17. oysters
18. clams
19. mussels
20. crab
21. lobster
22. shrimp
23. scallops

1. scrambled eggs
2. fried egg
3. cereal
4. pancakes
5. waffle
6. butter
7. muffin
8. doughnut/donut
9. toast
10. jelly/jam
11. bagel
12. chef's salad
13. fruit salad
14. soup
15. hamburger
16. hot dog
17. pizza
18. sandwich
19. fried chicken
20. french fries

21. submarine sandwich/hero	**25.** fish	**31.** macaroni and cheese	**36.** mustard
22. meat loaf	**26.** taco	**32.** rice	**37.** relish
23. spaghetti and meatballs	**27.** burrito	**33.** noodles	**38.** potato chips
24. egg rolls	**28.** baked potato	**34.** ketchup/catsup	**39.** pretzels
	29. mashed potatoes	**35.** mayonaise	**40.** popcorn
	30. gravy		**41.** peanuts

DESSERTS

1. pie
2. pie a la mode
3. turnover
4. pastries
5. cake
6. cheesecake
7. cookies
8. brownies
9. ice cream
10. ice cream cone
11. sundae
12. sherbet
13. frozen yogurt
14. yogurt
15. custard
16. pudding
17. gelatin
18. strawberry shortcake
19. chocolate mousse
20. candy

DRINKS

1. water
2. seltzer water/ soda water
3. whole milk
4. chocolate milk
5. milk shake
6. cream
7. tea
8. iced tea
9. coffee
10. apple juice
11. orange juice
12. grapefruit juice
13. grape juice
14. pineapple juice
15. cranberry juice
16. lemonade
17. soda/pop
18. wine
19. beer

COMMUNITY

CITY

1. sidewalk
2. street
3. taxi
4. department store
5. apartment building
6. park
7. mosque
8. airport
9. train station/
   railroad station
10. bus station
11. office building
12. church
13. synagogue
14. pedestrian
15. curb
16. traffic light/traffic
    signal/stop light

17. gas pump
18. mailbox
19. gas station
20. playground
21. school
22. library
23. parking lot
24. museum
25. police station
26. jail/prison/
    correctional
    facility
27. university
28. bus stop
29. crosswalk
30. street sign
31. high school
32. hospital

COUNTRY

1. grass
2. farmhouse
3. barn
4. silo
5. stream/brook
6. bridge
7. road
8. trees
9. sky
10. clouds
11. sun
12. woods
13. lake
14. picnic

15. field/pasture
16. chicken
17. sheep
18. cow
19. orchard
20. goat
21. horse
22. fence
23. crops
24. farmer
25. tractor
26. plow
27. bale
28. well

OCCUPATIONS

1. carpenter
2. plumber
3. waiter
4. waitress
5. cook/chef
6. tailor
7. driver/chauffeur
8. barber
9. hair stylist/
   beautician
10. salesperson
11. electrician
12. locksmith
13. computer
    technician/
    programmer
14. accountant
15. security guard
16. engineer
17. pilot
18. mason
19. bricklayer
20. construction
    worker
21. police officer
22. sailor
23. soldier

24. farmer
25. mechanic
26. fire fighter
27. housekeeper/maid
28. baby sitter/day care provider
29. fisherman
30. doctor
31. dentist
32. travel agent
33. teacher
34. gardener
35. painter
36. factory worker
37. foreman/supervisor
38. pharmacist
39. florist
40. secretary
41. reporter
42. artist

SHOPPING CENTER

1. hardware store
2. furniture store
3. restaurant
4. ice cream stand
5. beauty salon/
   hairdresser's
6. drugstore/
   pharmacy
7. barber shop
8. electronics store
9. music store
10. supermarket/
    grocery store
11. liquor store
12. flower shop

SUPERMARKET

1. fish
2. poultry
3. meat
4. beverages
5. vegetables
6. fruit
7. scale
8. eggs
9. cheese
10. dairy products
11. bakery
12. deli counter
13. cereals
14. canned vegetables/fruits
15. baby food/supplies
16. health and beauty aids

17. detergents
18. cleaning supplies
19. frozen foods
20. video center
21. cashier
22. cash register
23. shopping bag
24. conveyor belt
25. receipt
26. manager
27. customer
28. shopping basket
29. shopping cart/ grocery cart
30. stock clerk
31. snack foods

DRUGSTORE

1. newspapers
2. magazines
3. greeting cards
4. film
5. film developing center
6. vitamins
7. medicines
8. druggist/ pharmacist
9. prescription
10. cosmetics
11. school supplies/ stationery
12. flashlight
13. batteries
14. gum/bubble gum
15. humidifier
16. hot water bottle
17. cotton
18. tissues
19. shaving cream
20. razors
21. thermometer
22. adhesive tape
23. band-aids
24. aspirin
25. toothpaste
26. cashier
27. maps

HARDWARE STORE

1. key making machine
2. keys
3. locks
4. paint brushes
5. paint
6. fans
7. shovel
8. rake
9. shelf

10. lawn mower
11. bricks
12. wood/lumber
13. garbage cans/ trash cans
14. screens
15. glass
16. tools
17. power saw
18. pegboard

19. wire
20. level
21. pliers
22. monkey wrench
23. saw
24. screwdriver
25. Phillips screwdriver
26. tape measure
27. hammer

28. electric drill
29. bits
30. chisel
31. nails
32. screws
33. plane
34. wrench
35. rope
36. toolbox

RESTAURANT

1. menu
2. waiter
3. tablecloth
4. table
5. candlestick
6. customer
7. ashtray
8. liquor
9. lighter
10. bar stool
11. bar
12. cigarette
13. bartender
14. hostess
15. flowers
16. vase
17. chair
18. waitress
19. tray
20. salad bar
21. booth
22. silverware
23. dish
24. bill/check
25. tip

1. letter
2. date
3. name
4. greeting/salutation
5. closing
6. signature
7. envelope
8. return address
9. postmark
10. stamp
11. address
12. zip code
13. postcard
14. overnight package/ Express Mail
15. package
16. string
17. label
18. tape
19. air mail letter
20. mail truck
21. mailbox
22. mail
23. postal clerk
24. book of stamps
25. roll of stamps
26. line (for mail service)
27. mailbag
28. mail carrier/ letter carrier
29. stamp machine
30. mail slot
31. post office boxes

OFFICE

1. desk
2. typewriter
3. typing paper
4. envelope
5. letters/mail
6. pencil sharpener
7. pencil
8. typist
9. copy machine/ photocopier
10. word processor
11. in-box
12. out-box
13. file folder
14. file drawer
15. file cabinet
16. water fountain
17. job openings/ job postings
18. bulletin board
19. coffee machine/ coffee maker
20. switchboard
21. telephone
22. message pad
23. pen
24. switchboard operator
25. calendar
26. dictionary
27. tape
28. tape dispenser
29. appointment book
30. Rolodex® file
31. computer
32. print-out
33. printer
34. stapler
35. secretary

1. bank book/pass book
2. coins/change
3. ATM (Automatic Teller Machine) card
4. bills
5. travelers check
6. credit card
7. identification/ driver's license
8. monthly statement
9. checkbook
10. check
11. withdrawal slip
12. deposit slip
13. automatic teller machine/cash machine
14. security guard
15. bank vault
16. bank officer
17. safety deposit box
18. teller
19. customer
20. drive-through window
21. loan officer

1. classroom
2. textbook
3. test(s)
4. grade(s)/score(s)
5. paper
6. desk
7. notebook
8. computer
9. hall
10. principal
11. locker
12. student
13. teacher
14. chalkboard/
    blackboard/board
15. clock
16. chalk
17. eraser
18. ruler
19. homework/
    assignment

1. campus
2. instructor/professor
3. administration building
4. dean
5. president
6. registrar/registration
7. transcript
8. library
9. dormitory
10. student union
11. degree
12. diploma
13. graduation/ commencement

PLAYGROUND

1. park
2. slide
3. swings/swing set
4. kite
5. wading pool
6. bench
7. jungle gym
8. scooter
9. shovel
10. child
11. pail
12. sand
13. sandbox
14. seesaw
15. bicycle
16. water fountain
17. jump rope
18. hopscotch
19. tricycle
20. skateboard

1. file card/catalog card
2. title
3. author
4. subject
5. call number
6. card catalog
7. dictionary
8. atlas
9. encyclopedia
10. globe
11. newspaper rack
12. newspaper
13. magazines
14. journals
15. periodicals section
16. microfilm reader
17. audio-visual section
18. records
19. microfiche machine
20. information desk
21. stacks
22. shelf
23. library card
24. library books
25. librarian
26. checkout desk
27. book return/book drop

POLICE

1. police station
2. prisoner
3. jail
4. warden
5. police officer
6. badge
7. gun holster
8. parking meter
9. ticket
10. meter maid
11. traffic cop
12. nightstick
13. police car
14. patrol officer
15. tow away zone

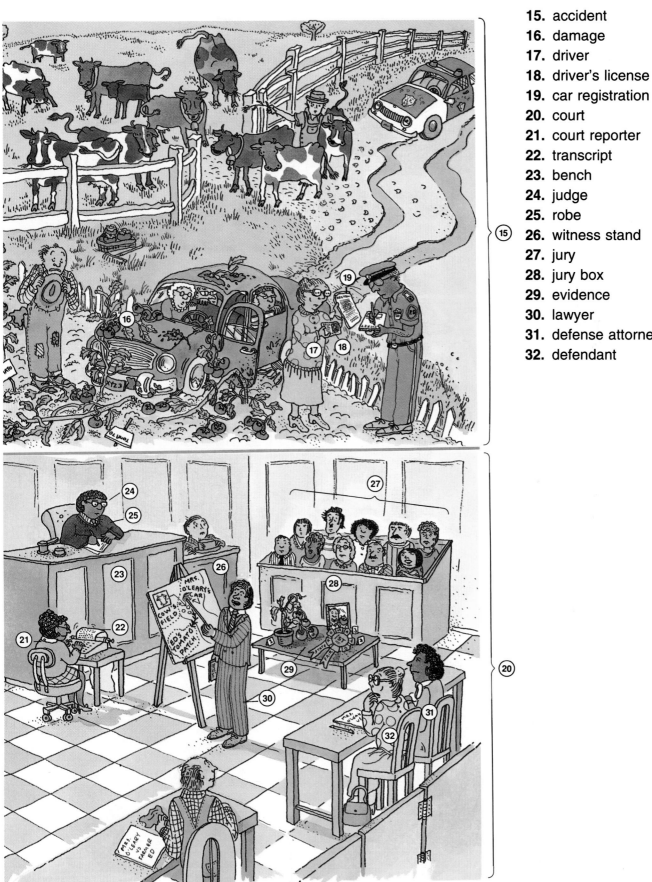

15. accident
16. damage
17. driver
18. driver's license
19. car registration
20. court
21. court reporter
22. transcript
23. bench
24. judge
25. robe
26. witness stand
27. jury
28. jury box
29. evidence
30. lawyer
31. defense attorney
32. defendant

1. fire
2. smoke detector
3. smoke
4. fire alarm
5. fire station
6. fire pole
7. fire engine
8. siren
9. fire chief
10. hook
11. ladder
12. ax
13. fire fighter

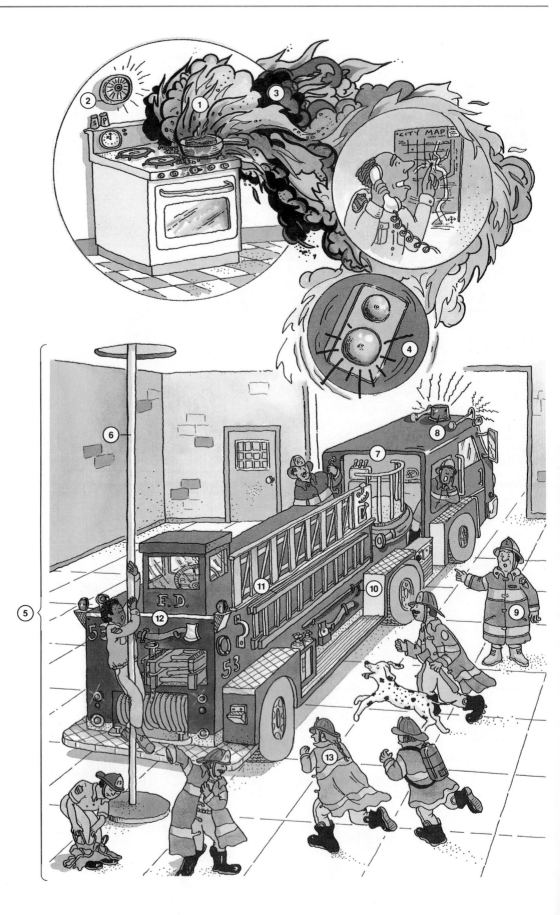

14. paramedic
15. fire hose
16. fire hydrant
17. ambulance
18. rescue
19. nozzle
20. fire extinguisher
21. coat
22. helmet
23. bull horn
24. ladder truck
25. water
26. fire escape

1. headache
2. cut/wound
3. stomach ache
4. fever
5. thermometer
6. cough
7. sore throat
8. itch
9. burn
10. sunburn
11. blister
12. break/fracture
13. rash
14. insect bite
15. toothache
16. backache
17. infection
18. bruise
19. cold

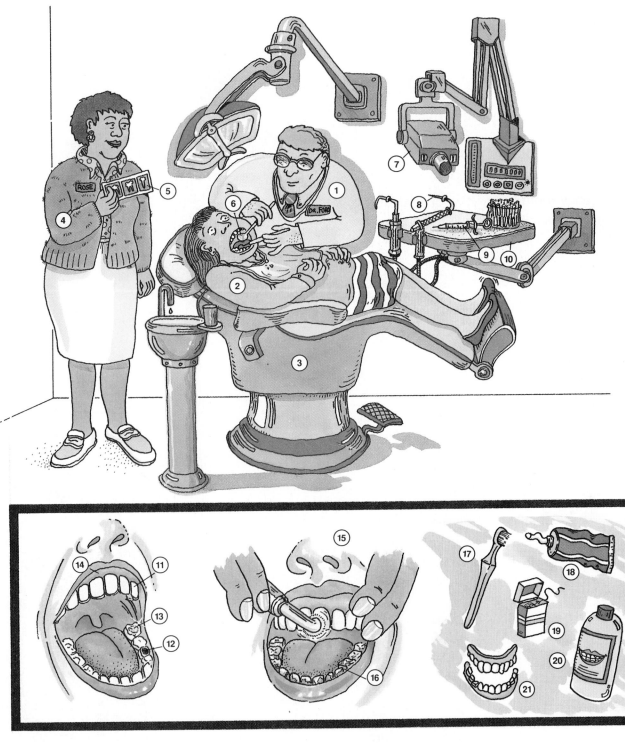

1. dentist
2. patient
3. dentist chair
4. dental hygienist/
   oral hygienist
5. X-ray

6. mirror
7. X-ray machine
8. drill
9. anesthetic
10. tray
11. tooth

12. cavity
13. filling
14. gums
15. cleaning
16. plaque/tartar
17. toothbrush

18. toothpaste
19. dental floss
20. mouthwash
21. false teeth/
    dentures

MEDICAL

1. doctor
2. stethoscope
3. blood pressure gauge
4. examination table
5. eye chart
6. scale
7. blood test
8. tongue depressors
9. prescription
10. emergency room
11. admitting desk
12. nurse
13. x-ray
14. sling
15. cast
16. stretcher/gurney
17. alcohol
18. cotton balls
19. bandage
20. medicine
21. needle
22. syringe

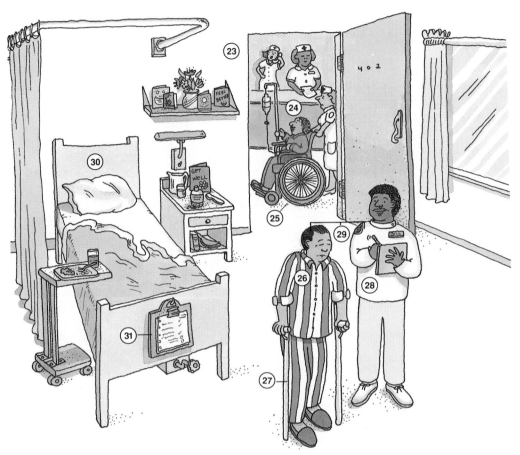

23. hospital room
24. nurse's station
25. wheelchair
26. patient
27. crutch
28. physical therapist
29. therapy
30. hospital bed
31. chart
32. operating room
33. intravenous (IV)
34. surgery
35. surgeon
36. monitor
37. surgical cap
38. mask
39. surgical nurse
40. instruments
41. anesthesiologist

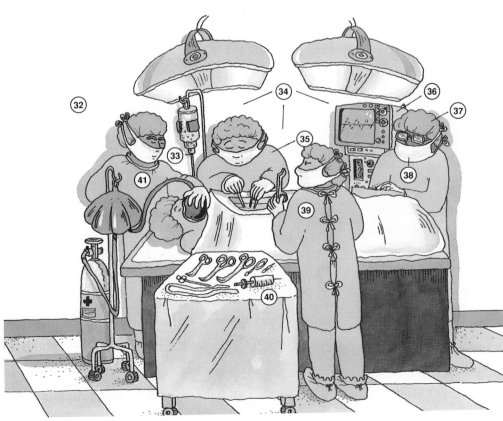

U.S. GOVERNMENT

Federal Government

1. President
2. White House
3. U.S. Capitol Building
4. Congress
5. Senate
6. House of Representatives
7. Supreme Court
8. Justices of the Supreme Court
9. Declaration of Independence

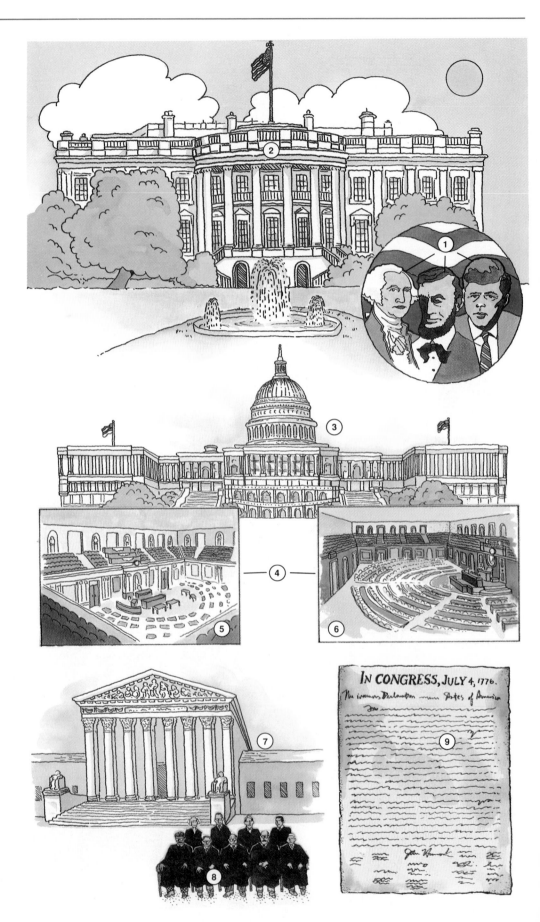

PETS

1. cat
2. kitten
3. dog
4. puppy
5. rabbit/bunny
6. French poodle
7. retriever
8. shepherd
9. terrier
10. canary
11. parrot
12. parakeet(s)
13. tropical fish
14. goldfish
15. mice
16. turtle
17. guinea pig
18. hamster(s)
19. gerbil(s)

FARM

1. cow
2. milk
3. bucket
4. calf

5. bull
6. chicken/hen
7. chick
8. eggs

9. rooster
10. duck
11. turkey
12. pig

13. pigpen/pig sty
14. piglet
15. goat

16. kid
17. sheep
18. lamb
19. horse
20. colt
21. donkey
22. barn
23. hay
24. hayloft
25. pitchfork
26. trough
27. skunk
28. tractor
29. shed

WILD ANIMALS

1. zebra
2. stripe
3. giraffe
4. elephant
5. trunk
6. tusk
7. camel
8. hump
9. kangaroo
10. pouch
11. lion
12. mane
13. leopard
14. spot
15. hyena
16. tiger
17. claw
18. monkey
19. tail
20. chimpanzee/chimp
21. baboon
22. gorilla
23. orangutan
24. bear
25. polar bear
26. panda
27. koala bear
28. wolf

29. deer
30. antler
31. llama
32. rhinoceros
33. hippopotamus
34. horn
35. buffalo/bison
36. fox
37. raccoon
38. porcupine
39. beaver
40. armadillo
41. anteater
42. bat
43. tortoise
44. frog
45. lizard
46. snake
47. alligator
48. crocodile
49. whale
50. dolphin
51. seal
52. otter
53. walrus
54. peacock
55. ostrich
56. owl
57. eagle
58. hawk

1. sparrow
2. swallow
3. hummingbird
4. blackbird
5. bluebird
6. blue jay
7. wing
8. feathers
9. beak
10. cuckoo
11. dove
12. pigeon
13. woodpecker
14. cardinal
15. robin
16. nest
17. egg
18. crow
19. goose
20. mallard
21. stork
22. bird of paradise
23. vulture
24. buzzard
25. roadrunner
26. pelican
27. bill
28. penguin
29. crane
30. flamingo
31. swan
32. sea gull

FISH AND SEA ANIMALS

1. octopus
2. tentacle
3. jellyfish
4. squid
5. starfish
6. shark
7. snout
8. fin
9. tail
10. trout
11. gill
12. perch
13. catfish
14. bass
15. angelfish
16. eel
17. hake
18. flying fish
19. barracuda
20. sailfish
21. herring
22. whitefish
23. scale

INSECTS AND RODENTS

Insects

1. ant
2. anthill
3. bee
4. honeycomb
5. hive
6. beetle
7. butterfly
8. wing
9. caterpillar
10. cocoon
11. centipede
12. cicada
13. locust
14. cockroach/roach
15. cricket
16. dragonfly
17. firefly/lightning bug
18. flea
19. gnat
20. grasshopper
21. ladybug
22. mosquito
23. moth
24. praying mantis
25. scorpion
26. stinger
27. spider
28. web
29. termite
30. walking stick
31. wasp

Rodents

32. squirrel
33. chipmunk
34. mouse
35. rat
36. gopher

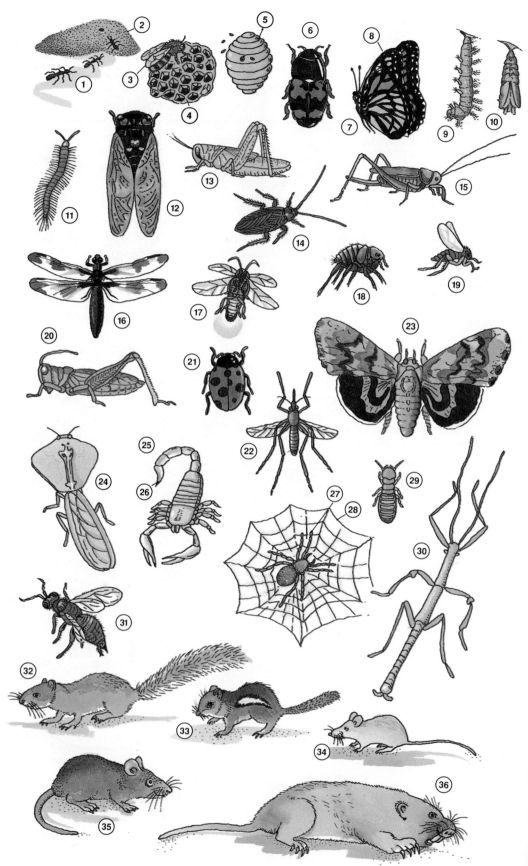

PLANTS AND TREES

1. tree
2. sapling
3. branch
4. twig
5. leaf
6. bark
7. trunk
8. root

9. sap
10. cactus
11. redwood
12. palm
13. magnolia
14. oak
15. acorn
16. maple

17. pine tree
18. cone
19. needle
20. elm
21. birch
22. willow
23. poplar
24. eucalyptus

25. bush
26. vine
27. house plant/
    potted plant
28. fern
29. weed
30. herbs

FLOWERS

1. tulip	**8.** pansy	**15.** petunia	**22.** violet
2. bulb	**9.** iris	**16.** daffodil	**23.** sunflower
3. rose	**10.** orchid	**17.** crocus	**24.** petal
4. thorn	**11.** daisy	**18.** hyacinth	**25.** bouquet
5. stem	**12.** chrysanthemum	**19.** zinnia	**26.** corsage
6. bud	**13.** buttercup	**20.** gardenia	**27.** wreath
7. lily	**14.** marigold	**21.** poinsettia	**28.** greenhouse/nursery

AIRPORT

1. terminal building
2. control tower
3. airplane/plane/jet
4. nose
5. landing gear
6. wing
7. cargo door
8. cargo area
9. fuselage
10. engine
11. tail
12. hangar
13. runway
14. blimp
15. glider
16. propeller plane
17. helicopter
18. rotor

1. parking garage
2. terminal
3. sky cap/porter
4. suitcase
5. garment bag
6. check-in counter/ ticket counter
7. ticket agent
8. conveyor belt
9. passport
10. visa
11. boarding pass
12. ticket
13. security guard
14. waiting area
15. gate
16. arrival/departure board
17. x-ray screener
18. metal detector
19. passenger
20. cockpit
21. captain
22. co-pilot

23. instrument panel
24. flight engineer/
     navigator
25. cabin
26. movie
27. life vest
28. oxygen mask
29. sick bag
30. lavatory
31. flight attendant
32. beverage cart

33. aisle
34. tray
35. window
36. seat number
37. overhead
     compartment

38. economy class
39. first class
40. earphone
41. armrest
42. seat belt

43. baggage claim
44. baggage
45. ground
     transportation

1. bicycle
2. handlebars
3. hand brake
4. seat
5. brake
6. chain
7. sprocket
8. pedal
9. bicycle pump
10. gear changer
11. cable
12. tire
13. spoke
14. reflector
15. lock
16. tricycle
17. motorcycle
18. helmet
19. engine
20. shock absorbers
21. exhaust pipe
22. scooter
23. recreational vehicle/RV/ camper
24. car
25. airplane
26. boat
27. ship
28. dock
29. ferry

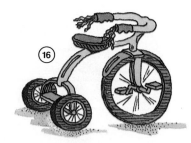

CARS AND TRUCKS

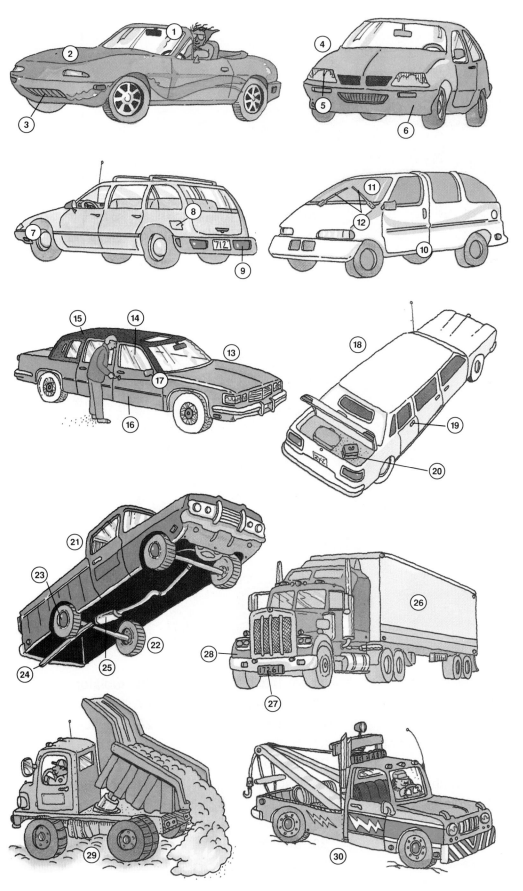

1. convertible
2. hood
3. grill
4. compact
5. lights
6. bumper
7. station wagon
8. gas tank
9. tail light
10. mini-van
11. windshield
12. windshield wiper
13. sedan
14. window
15. top
16. door
17. lock
18. limousine
19. handle
20. trunk
21. pick-up truck
22. tire
23. hubcap
24. tail pipe/exhaust pipe
25. muffler
26. tractor trailer
27. license plate
28. fender
29. dump truck
30. tow truck

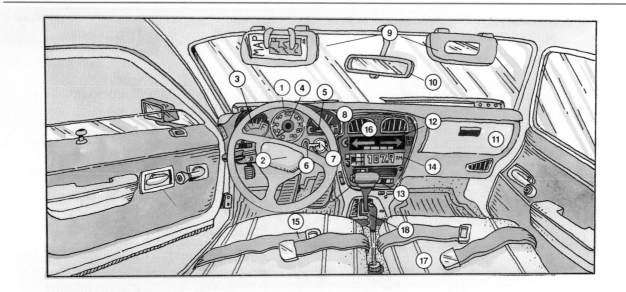

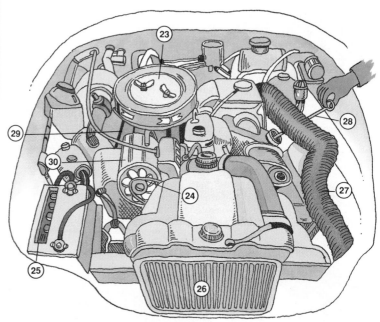

Automatic Transmission

1. steering wheel
2. horn
3. fuel gauge
4. speedometer
5. temperature gauge
6. key
7. ignition
8. instrument panel/ dashboard

9. visor(s)
10. rearview mirror
11. glove compartment
12. heater
13. gearshift
14. radio
15. seat belt
16. air conditioner
17. seat
18. emergency brake

Manual Transmission

19. stick shift
20. clutch
21. brake
22. gas pedal/ accelerator

Engine

23. air filter
24. fan belt
25. battery

26. radiator
27. hose
28. dipstick
29. motor
30. alternator
31. spare tire
32. jack

PUBLIC TRANSPORTATION

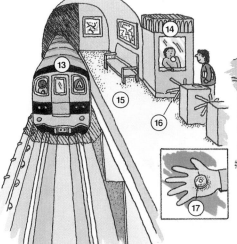

1. bus
2. bus stop
3. bus driver
4. fare box
5. cord
6. taxi/cab
7. off-duty sign
8. license plate
9. cab driver
10. fare
11. meter
12. passenger
13. subway
14. token booth
15. platform
16. turnstile
17. token
18. train
19. train station
20. conductor
21. commuter
22. engineer
23. ticket counter
24. ticket
25. train schedule
26. track
27. trolley/streetcar

Road Travel

1. stop sign
2. traffic light
3. go
4. caution
5. stop
6. yield
7. one way to the right
8. one way to the left
9. right turn only
10. left turn only
11. no right turn
12. no left turn
13. do not enter
14. no parking
15. handicapped parking
16. no U turn
17. no passing
18. crosswalk
19. pedestrian crossing
20. school zone/ school crossing
21. railroad crossing
22. speed limit sign

Highway Travel

23. overpass
24. underpass
25. left lane/passing lane
26. center lane/middle lane
27. right lane
28. cloverleaf
29. solid line
30. broken line
31. toll booth
32. exit ramp
33. route sign

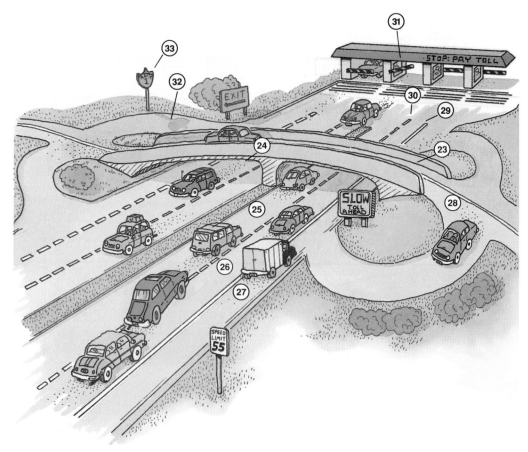

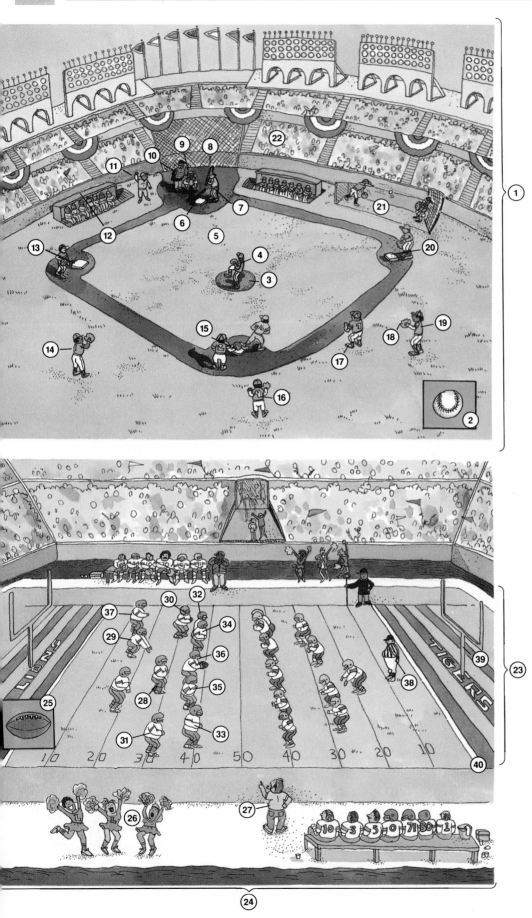

Professional Sports

Baseball

1. baseball park
2. baseball
3. pitcher's mound
4. pitcher
5. baseball diamond
6. home plate
7. batter
8. bat
9. catcher
10. umpire
11. manager
12. dugout
13. first base
14. right fielder
15. second base
16. center fielder
17. shortstop
18. glove/mitt
19. left fielder
20. third base
21. bullpen
22. stands

Football

23. football field
24. stadium
25. football
26. cheerleaders
27. coach
28. quarterback
29. halfback
30. tight end
31. split end
32. left tackle
33. right tackle
34. left guard
35. right guard
36. center
37. flanker
38. referee
39. goal post
40. end zone

Basketball

1. basketball court
2. basketball player
3. basketball
4. basket

Ice Hockey

5. ice rink/
   hockey rink
6. hockey player
7. skate
8. hockey stick
9. puck
10. glove
11. mask
12. goalie
13. net

Soccer

14. soccer player
15. soccer ball
16. soccer field
17. goal

Tennis

18. tennis court
19. tennis ball
20. tennis racket
21. net (tennis court)
22. tennis player

Wrestling

23. wrestler
24. mat

Boxing

25. boxing ring
26. boxer
27. boxing glove
28. referee

Volleyball

29. volleyball court
30. net (volleyball)
31. volleyball
32. volleyball player

Horse Racing

33. horsetrack
34. jockey
35. saddle
36. reins
37. gate

1. golf
2. golf ball
3. golf club
4. tee
5. green
6. fairway
7. golf bag
8. softball
9. ping-pong/table tennis
10. paddle
11. ping-pong ball
12. badminton
13. horseback riding
14. bicycle riding/cycling
15. bowling
16. bowling ball
17. bowling alley
18. lane
19. gutter
20. pins
21. croquet
22. hiking
23. backpack
24. mountain climbing
25. aerobics
26. jogging
27. nautilus/weight lifting
28. barbell/weight lifting
29. hunting
30. gun
31. lacrosse
32. karate
33. racquetball
34. racquet
35. handball
36. handball court
37. track and field
38. runner
39. gymnastics
40. gymnast(s)
41. balance beam

WATER SPORTS AND WINTER SPORTS

Swimming
1. swimming pool
2. swimmer

Diving
3. diving board
4. diver

Crew/Rowing
5. crew
6. oars
7. boat

Canoeing
8. canoe
9. paddle

Kayaking
10. kayak

Water Skiing
11. water skis
12. towrope
13. speed boat

Surfing
14. surfboard
15. wave/surf
16. surfer

Sailing
17. sailboat
18. mast
19. sailor

Windsurfing
20. windsurf sail

Snorkeling
21. snorkel

Scuba Diving
22. scuba diver
23. air tank
24. mask
25. wet suit

Fishing
26. fishing line
27. fishing rod

Ice Skating
28. skate
29. ice
30. skater

Sledding
31. sled
32. toboggan
33. bobsled

Downhill Alpine Skiing
34. ski pole
35. ski(s)
36. skier
37. chairlift/lift

Cross-Country Skiing
38. trail
39. cross-country skis

Snowmobiling
40. snowmobile

SPORTS VERBS

1. kick
2. catch
3. throw
4. pass
5. ice skate
6. score (a goal)
7. ski

8. slide
9. dive
10. swim
11. fight
12. roller skate
13. bowl
14. fence

15. wrestle
16. ride
17. jog/run
18. bounce/dribble
19. jump
20. serve
21. surf

22. drive
23. win (the game)
24. lose (the game)
25. tie (the game)
26. keep score

LEISURE TIME ACTIVITIES

1. dancing
2. roller skating
3. exercising
4. shopping
5. walking
6. reading
7. camping
8. picnic (have a)
9. movies (go to)
10. zoo (go to)
11. museum (go to)
12. vacation (take a)
13. beach (go to)
14. lifeguard
15. sunglasses
16. beach towel
17. seashells
18. sand
19. beach umbrella
20. beach chair
21. swimsuit/bathing
    suit
22. swim trunks
23. waves

HOBBIES AND CRAFTS

1. painting
2. canvas
3. sculpting
4. sculpture
5. pottery
6. clay
7. potter's wheel
8. knitting
9. yarn
10. knitting needle
11. sewing
12. fabric
13. sewing machine
14. embroidery
15. hoop
16. thread
17. scissors
18. crocheting
19. crochet hook
20. stamp collecting
21. album
22. coin collecting
23. bird watching
24. playing cards

Audio

1. stereo system
2. turntable
3. needle
4. arm
5. receiver
6. volume knob
7. headphones
8. tape player/
   cassette player
9. compact disc
   player
10. compact disc
11. tape/cassette
12. records
13. speaker

Visual

14. television/TV
15. video cassette
    recorder/VCR
16. videocassette/tape
17. video camera
18. movie camera
19. movie projector
20. film reel

Photography

21. camera
22. roll of film
23. lens
24. flash
25. zoom lens
26. prints
27. slides

PARTY AND DANCE

1. invitation
2. host
3. hostess
4. guests
5. laughing
6. introducing
7. shaking hands
8. eating
9. refreshments
10. playing games
11. disc jockey/DJ
12. stereo system
13. tapes
14. compact discs
15. records
16. dancing

PERFORMING ARTS

Rock Concert

1. nightclub
2. rock band
3. lead singer
4. electric guitar (ist)
5. drummer
6. bass guitar (ist)
7. keyboard
8. synthesizer

Play

9. theater
10. scenery
11. spotlight
12. actor
13. actress
14. stage
15. curtain
16. balcony
17. usher
18. audience
19. seats

Symphony Concert

20. auditorium/
    concert hall
21. orchestra
22. conductor
23. baton
24. music stand
25. musician

Ballet

26. ballerina
27. ballet dancer
28. toe shoe
29. tutu
30. footlights

MUSICAL INSTRUMENTS

Brass
1. trumpet
2. trombone
3. French horn
4. tuba

Woodwinds
5. flute
6. piccolo
7. recorder
8. clarinet
9. bassoon
10. oboe
11. saxophone

Percussion
12. drum
13. drumsticks
14. cymbals
15. tambourine
16. conga drum
17. kettledrum
18. bongo drums
19. xylophone

Strings
20. violin
21. bow
22. viola
23. cello
24. guitar
25. bass
26. harp
27. mandolin
28. ukelele
29. banjo
30. piano

Other Instruments
31. organ
32. harmonica
33. accordian

WEDDING

Marriage Ceremony

1. bride
2. groom/bridegroom
3. wedding dress
4. veil
5. bouquet
6. tuxedo
7. boutonniere
8. best man
9. maid of honor
10. bridesmaid
11. ring bearer
12. wedding rings
13. flower girl
14. justice of the peace
15. engagement ring/ diamond
16. marriage license
17. wedding invitation

Reception

18. head table
19. guests
20. wedding cake
21. banquet

BIRTHDAYS

1. birthday party
2. birthday card
3. birthday cake
4. candles
5. blow out (the candles)
6. make a wish
7. balloons
8. party hat
9. refreshments
10. favors
11. guests
12. gift/present
13. gift wrap
14. bow
15. magician
16. hat
17. rabbit

CHRISTMAS

1. Christmas tree
2. ornaments
3. garland
4. tinsel
5. gifts
6. holly
7. fireplace
8. stocking
9. wreath
10. lights
11. carolers
12. Christmas cards
13. Santa Claus
14. sack
15. beard
16. cap
17. sleigh
18. reindeer
19. bells

NEW YEAR'S EVE

CHINESE NEW YEAR

1. party
2. clock
3. stroke of midnight
4. streamers
5. noise maker

6. confetti
7. party hat
8. toast
9. champagne
10. fireworks

11. Chinese dragon
12. parade
13. banner (Happy New Year in Chinese)
14. marchers

HALLOWEEN

1. pumpkin
2. jack-o-lantern
3. candle
4. trick or treater
5. treats
6. mask
7. broomstick
8. (trick or treater) bag

Costumes

9. witch
10. clown
11. flower
12. mummy
13. pirate
14. skeleton
15. ghost
16. tiger
17. princess
18. devil

19. costume party
20. decorations
21. bat
22. black cat
23. apple
24. apple bob/bobbing for apples
25. tub
26. candy

THANKSGIVING

1. Thanksgiving dinner
2. turkey
3. carving knife
4. cranberry sauce
5. stuffing
6. apple cider
7. pumpkin pie
8. pilgrims
9. Mayflower
10. Native Americans
11. horn of plenty/ cornucopia

10 THE UNIVERSE AND THE WORLD

THE UNIVERSE

1. star
2. comet
3. tail
4. North Star
5. Little Dipper
6. Big Dipper
7. constellation
8. planets
9. Sun
10. Mercury
11. Venus
12. Earth
13. Moon

14. asteroid
15. shooting star
16. meteor
17. Mars
18. Jupiter
19. Saturn
20. rings
21. Uranus
22. Neptune
23. Pluto
24. Milky Way
25. orbit

GEOGRAPHY

1. Earth
2. continent
3. ocean
4. sea
5. North Pole
6. longitude
7. latitude
8. equator
9. South Pole
10. gulf
11. hemisphere(s)
12. island
13. peninsula
14. bay
15. river
16. plain
17. lake
18. hill
19. valley
20. mountain

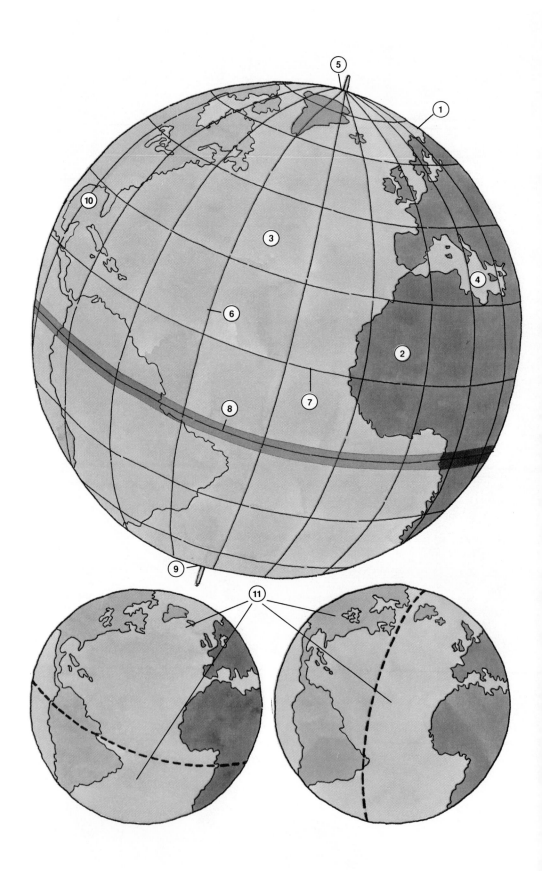

U.S. MAP

1. Washington
2. Oregon
3. California
4. Alaska
5. Arizona
6. Nevada
7. Utah
8. Idaho
9. Montana
10. Wyoming
11. Colorado
12. New Mexico
13. Hawaii
14. Texas
15. Oklahoma
16. Kansas
17. Nebraska
18. South Dakota
19. North Dakota
20. Minnesota
21. Wisconsin
22. Iowa
23. Illinois
24. Missouri
25. Arkansas
26. Louisiana
27. Mississippi

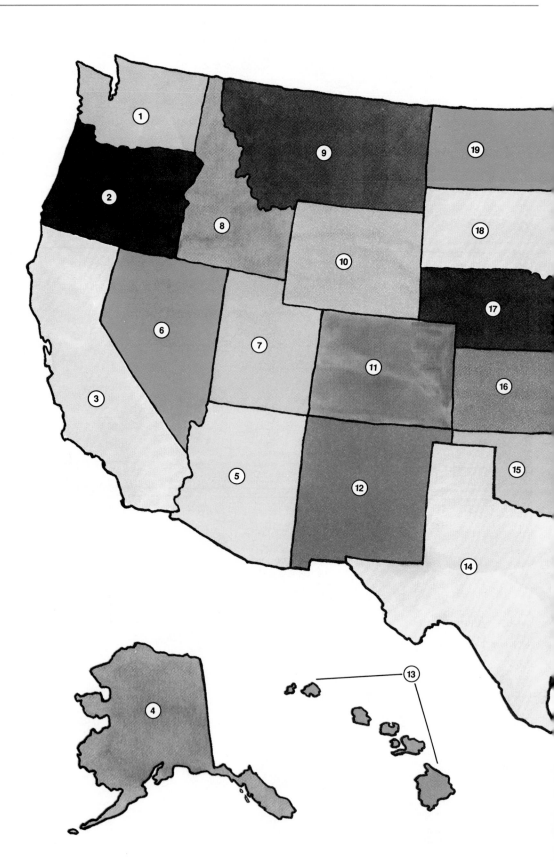

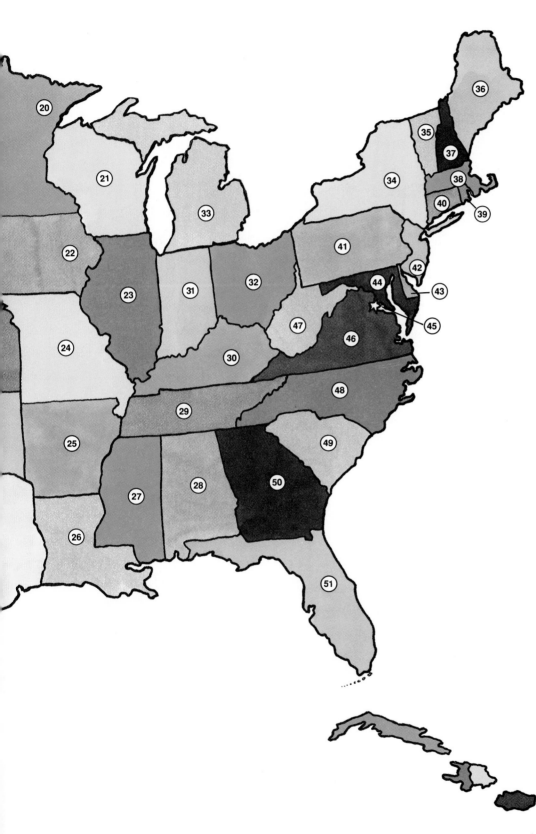

28. Alabama
29. Tennessee
30. Kentucky
31. Indiana
32. Ohio
33. Michigan
34. New York
35. Vermont
36. Maine
37. New Hampshire
38. Massachusetts
39. Rhode Island
40. Connecticut
41. Pennsylvania
42. New Jersey
43. Delaware
44. Maryland
45. Washington, D.C.
46. Virginia
47. West Virginia
48. North Carolina
49. South Carolina
50. Georgia
51. Florida
52. Puerto Rico

THE AMERICAS

North America
1. Canada
2. United States
3. Mexico

The Caribbean
4. Cuba
5. Haiti
6. Dominican Republic
7. Puerto Rico

Central America
8. Guatemala
9. Belize
10. Honduras
11. El Salvador
12. Costa Rica
13. Nicaragua
14. Panama

South America
15. Guyana
16. Venezuela
17. Colombia
18. Ecuador
19. Peru
20. Brazil
21. Bolivia
22. Paraguay
23. Chile
24. Argentina
25. Uruguay

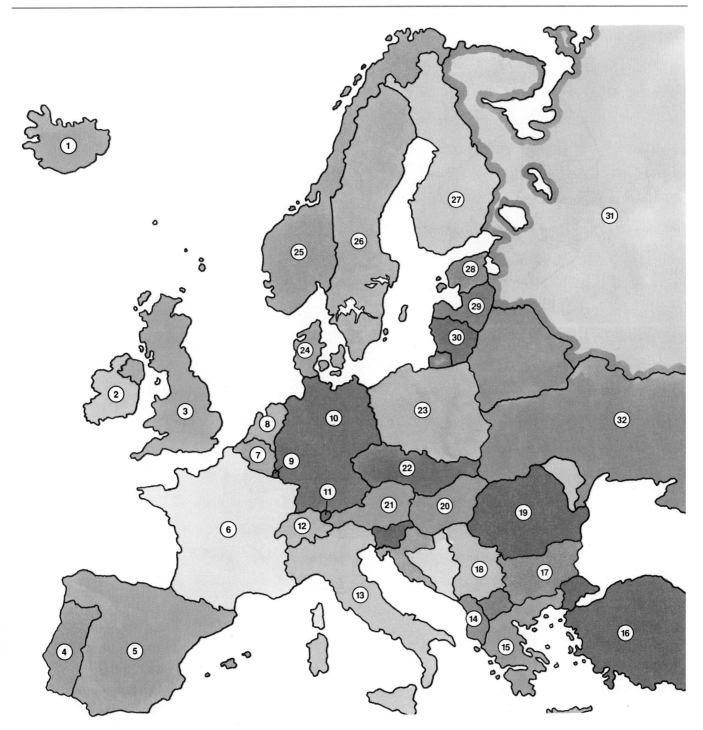

1. Iceland	**8.** Netherlands	**17.** Bulgaria	**25.** Norway
2. Ireland	**9.** Luxembourg	**18.** Yugoslavia	**26.** Sweden
3. United Kingdom of Great Britain and Northern Ireland	**10.** Germany	**19.** Romania	**27.** Finland
	11. Liechtenstein	**20.** Hungary	**28.** Estonia
	12. Switzerland	**21.** Austria	**29.** Latvia
4. Portugal	**13.** Italy	**22.** Czechoslovakia*	**30.** Lithuania
5. Spain	**14.** Albania	**23.** Poland	**31.** Russia
6. France	**15.** Greece	**24.** Denmark	**32.** Ukraine
7. Belgium	**16.** Turkey		

*Czechoslovakia has been divided into the Czech Republic and Slovakia.

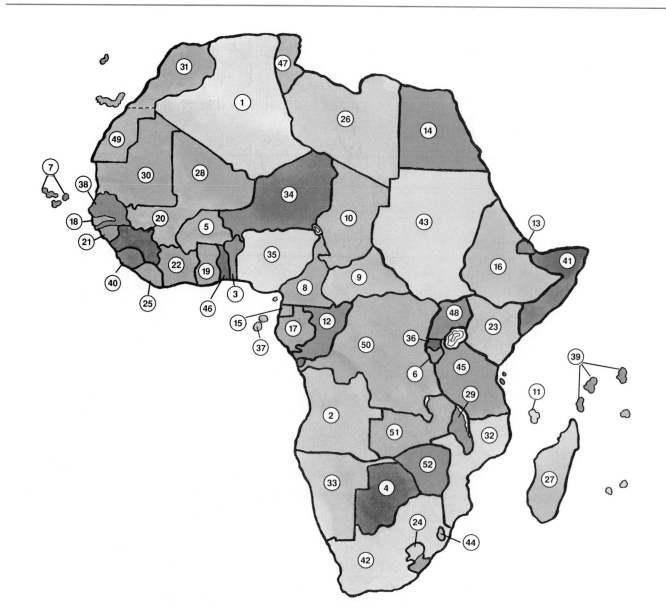

1. Algeria	**14.** Egypt	**28.** Mali	**41.** Somalia
2. Angola	**15.** Equatorial Guinea	**29.** Malawi	**42.** South Africa
3. Benin	**16.** Ethiopia	**30.** Mauritania	**43.** Sudan
4. Botswana	**17.** Gabon	**31.** Morocco	**44.** Swaziland
5. Burkina Faso	**18.** Gambia	**32.** Mozambique	**45.** Tanzania
6. Burundi	**19.** Ghana	**33.** Namibia	**46.** Togo
7. Cameroon	**20.** Guinea	**34.** Niger	**47.** Tunisia
8. Cape Verde	**21.** Guinea Bissau	**35.** Nigeria	**48.** Uganda
9. Central African	**22.** Ivory Coast	**36.** Rwanda	**49.** Western Sahara
Republic	**23.** Kenya	**37.** Sao tome	**50.** Zaire
10. Chad	**24.** Lesotho	y Principe	**51.** Zambia
11. Comoros	**25.** Liberia	**38.** Senegal	**52.** Zimbabwe
12. Congo	**26.** Libya	**39.** Seychelles	
13. Djibouti	**27.** Madagascar	**40.** Sierra Leone	

ASIA AND AUSTRALIA

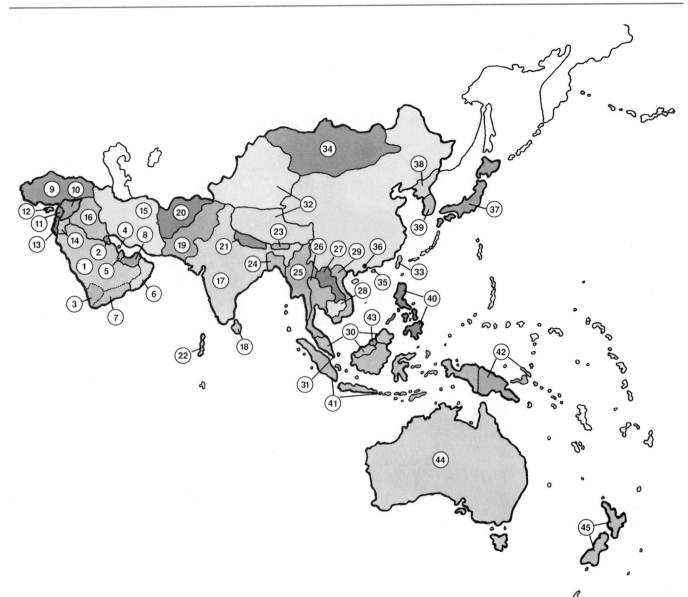

Asia

1. Saudi Arabia
2. Kuwait
3. Yemen Arab Republic
4. Bahrain
5. Qatar
6. Oman
7. People's Democratic Republic of Yemen
8. United Arab Emirates
9. Turkey
10. Syria
11. Lebanon
12. Cyprus
13. Israel
14. Jordan
15. Iran
16. Iraq
17. India
18. Sri Lanka/Ceylon
19. Pakistan
20. Afghanistan
21. Nepal
22. Maldives
23. Bhutan
24. Bangladesh
25. Burma
26. Thailand
27. Laos
28. Cambodia
29. Vietnam
30. Malaysia
31. Singapore
32. China
33. Taiwan
34. Mongolia
35. Hong Kong
36. Macau
37. Japan
38. North Korea
39. South Korea
40. Philippines
41. Indonesia
42. Papua New Guinea
43. Brunei
44. Australia
45. New Zealand

THE WORLD

Continents
1. North America
2. South America
3. Antarctica
4. Europe
5. Africa
6. Asia
7. Australia

Oceans
8. Antarctic
9. Indian
10. Pacific
11. Arctic
12. Atlantic

Mountains
13. Rocky Mountains
14. Sierra Madre
15. Andes
16. Atlas
17. Alps
18. Urals
19. Caucasus
20. Himalayas

Deserts
21. Gobi
22. Sahara

Bays, Lakes, Gulfs, Seas
23. Hudson Bay
24. Great Lakes
25. Gulf of Alaska
26. Gulf of Mexico
27. Caribbean Sea
28. North Sea
29. Baltic Sea
30. Black Sea
31. Caspian Sea
32. Mediterranean
    Sea

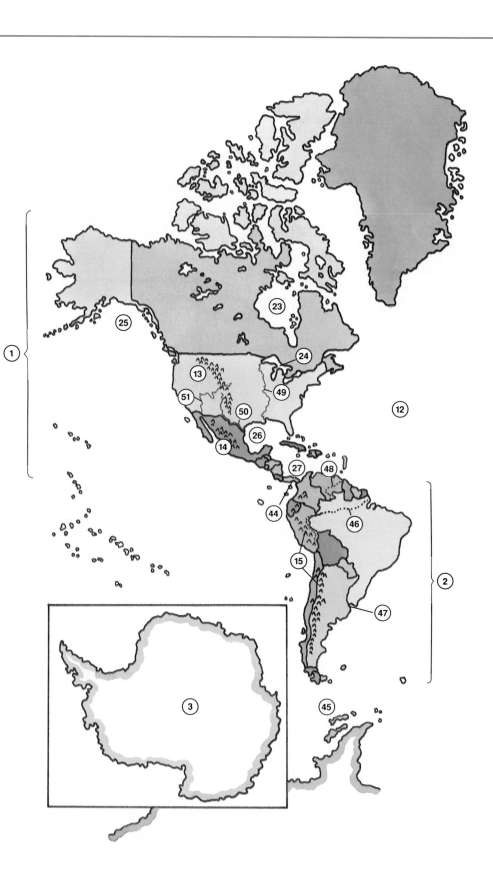

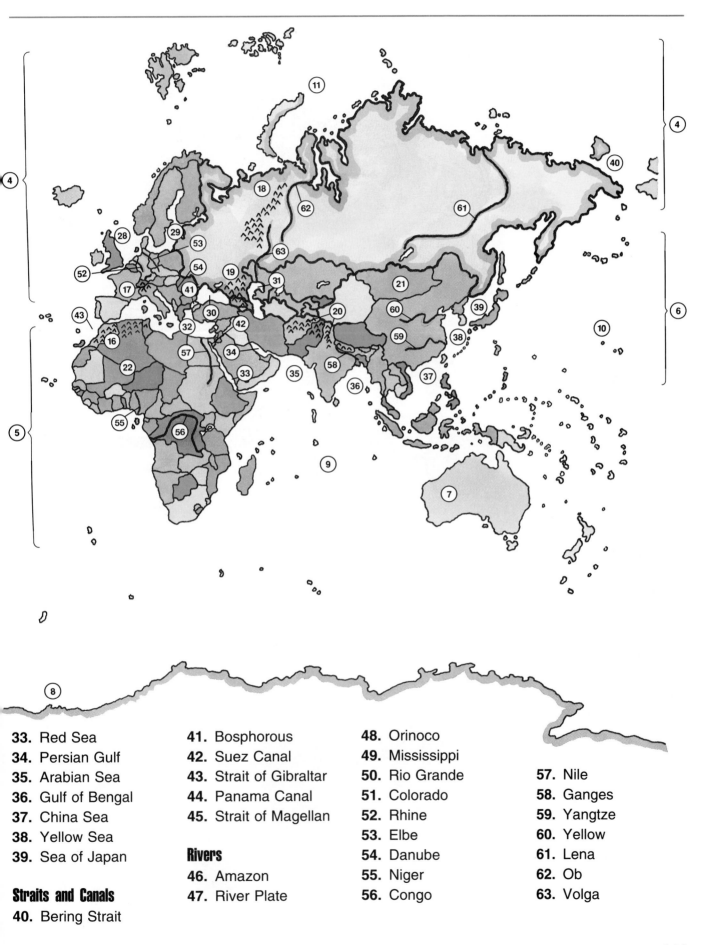

33. Red Sea
34. Persian Gulf
35. Arabian Sea
36. Gulf of Bengal
37. China Sea
38. Yellow Sea
39. Sea of Japan

Straits and Canals
40. Bering Strait

41. Bosphorous
42. Suez Canal
43. Strait of Gibraltar
44. Panama Canal
45. Strait of Magellan

Rivers
46. Amazon
47. River Plate

48. Orinoco
49. Mississippi
50. Rio Grande
51. Colorado
52. Rhine
53. Elbe
54. Danube
55. Niger
56. Congo

57. Nile
58. Ganges
59. Yangtze
60. Yellow
61. Lena
62. Ob
63. Volga

MEASURES

Size
1. big
2. bigger
3. biggest
4. small
5. smaller
6. smallest
7. short
8. shorter
9. shortest
10. tall
11. taller
12. tallest

Weight
13. heavy
14. light

Length
15. short
16. long

Width
17. wide
18. narrow

Volume
19. cup
20. pint
21. quart
22. gallon

Depth
23. shallow
24. deep

Speed
25. fast
26. slow

SEASONS AND WEATHER

Seasons
1. fall
2. winter
3. spring
4. summer

Weather
5. cloudy
6. rainy
7. sunny
8. hot
9. cold
10. windy
11. snow
12. hail
13. tornado
14. hurricane
15. thunder
16. lightning

THE CALENDAR AND NUMBERS

Months

1. January
2. February
3. March
4. April
5. May
6. June
7. July
8. August
9. September
10. October
11. November
12. December

Days

13. Sunday
14. Monday
15. Tuesday
16. Wednesday
17. Thursday
18. Friday
19. Saturday

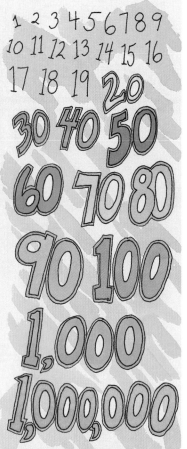

Numbers

1	one	11	eleven	30	thirty
2	two	12	twelve	40	forty
3	three	13	thirteen	50	fifty
4	four	14	fourteen	60	sixty
5	five	15	fifteen	70	seventy
6	six	16	sixteen	80	eighty
7	seven	17	seventeen	90	ninety
8	eight	18	eighteen	100	one hundred
9	nine	19	nineteen	1000	one thousand
10	ten	20	twenty	1,000,000	one million

PREPOSITIONS OF PLACE

1. at (the door)
2. in front of (the house)
3. beside (the house)
4. on (the table)
5. under (the table)
6. in (the trunk)
7. inside (the cage)
8. outside (the cage)
9. in back of (the house)
10. out of (the house)
11. through (the yard)
12. over (the fence)
13. across (the street)
14. above (the house)
15. below (the clouds)
16. beyond (the horizon)
17. near (the tree)
18. far from (the house)
19. around (the flag pole)
20. into (the dog house)
21. from (the fence)
22. to (the bush)

WORD LIST

122